BEHIND

THE SCENES

Dedicated to George Victor Bennett

BEHIND

THE SCENES

in the view of photographer

CHRIS BENNETT

André Deutsch

ACKNOWLEDGEMENTS

Chris Bennett would like to thank all staff at Harrods who, without exception, were courteous, helpful and enthusiastic at all times. It is their unparalleled spirit that helps to make Harrods the ultimate shopping experience.

It would be impossible to acknowledge everyone who contributed time and effort directly or indirectly into the production of this book, but we would especially like to thank those who went that extra mile to make this project a reality. A sincere thank you to Mohamed Al Fayed for allowing us unprecedented access to his very special Palace in Knightsbridge; to Peter Willasey, Vanessa Rome, Michael Mann, Gill Christophers and all the highly efficient members of the Harrods Press Office; to Chris Kirby and Sharla Franklin of Brand Management; to David West and the resplendent Harrods Horses Team; to Stephen Wheeler, Chris Lester and Simon Young from Harrods nerve centre – the kitchens; Sebastian Wormell and Lottie Clark of Company Archive and to Laurie Mayer, Bill Mitchell, Emad Estafanous, Giuseppe Silvestre, Richard Furnival-Jones and Rodney.

A very special thanks must go to Christianne Sherwen. Without her belief and enthusiasm this book might never have become a reality. And lastly an equally special thanks to Stella Scordellis, without whom the idea might never have been born.

First published in Great Britain in 1999 by
André Deutsch Ltd 76 Dean Street London W1V 5HA
www.vci.co.uk

This work is published by arrangement with Harrods Limited

Photographs copyright © Chris Bennett 1999

All photographs contained in this book were shot on Kodak Elitechrome film stock using Nikon and Minolta camera equipment. Processing by Ceta, Poland Street, London W1

ISBN 0-233-99617-6

Book design by Design/Section, Frome, Somerset
Reprographics by Radstock Reproductions, Midsomer Norton, Bath
Printed and bound in the UK by Butler & Tanner Limited, Frome and London

Introduction

It was with a degree of trepidation that during the second half of 1998 I began photography for *Harrods: Behind the Scenes*, the book you now hold. As a photographer with fourteen picture-led books published, until then the vast majority of my projects had centred on overtly dynamic subjects, subjects such as jet-fighter aircraft and Formula One motor racing. Seemingly for me, the faster, the noisier, the better. Could I convert my skills as an 'action' photographer to do justice to such a national institution as Harrods?

The notion for such a book first came about during a visit to Knightsbridge with my good friend and colleague Stella Scordellis for the January Sale in 1998. When she suggested that I should produce a book on Harrods, my initial reaction was scepticism. How could one create a dynamic picture-led book about a shop?

But it's surprising how blinkered we can be. Just a few minutes of really looking was all that was necessary to convince me that Stella might be right; the wealth of lavish artistry and everyday action within Harrods could indeed combine to provide the nucleus for a book which would surprise and beguile.

Nearly all the books that I have produced over the past decade have possessed a strong 'behind the scenes' and, as I term it, 'people and action' slant. Be it working with the Red Arrows, a Formula One team or sailing aboard a US Navy aircraft carrier, I had several aims in view. In addition to portraying the more obvious hardware itself, my task was to capture spontaneous imagery of the personnel at work and my challenge to encapsulate the true life and spirit of my subject. To achieve this and to record the reality, it is essential that I become trusted and accepted by my subject, ideally almost becoming one of the 'team'. It really is only then that one can attain the relaxed freedom necessary to capture this true spirit on film.

Harrods: Behind the Scenes was created over a period of nine months. Working generally for one day in every week, the fifth floor-based Press Office enthusiastically helped to schedule events and guide me through the labyrinth that is Harrods.

At first I was escorted at all times, particularly on the shop floor where, mingling with shoppers, quite uniquely I was granted permission to set up my tripod and take pictures even during opening hours. The resulting images thereby possess the essential ingredient which brings the store alive – the human element. Before long, a mutual trust developed and I was allowed to negotiate the floors unaccompanied, such freedom only enhancing my enjoyment of the subject.

Although this book is entitled 'behind the scenes', in reality it is a mix of public and private, a mix of what visitors to this veritable palace in Knightsbridge do see and what they don't. And, for the picture-hungry creative photographer, a palace is indeed what Harrods proved to be, an incredible Aladdin's Cave of brilliantly colourful and uniquely decorative displays. I loved the Egyptian Escalators, the Egyptian Rooms, the Food Halls, restaurants and award-winning Friesian horses with their ancient, gleaming delivery carriages. And I found fascinating the spotless kitchens, the Trevor Square stables, the security, the subterranean 'engine' room and the warehouses at Osterley.

As well as attempting to introduce a largely unseen side of Harrods to visitors and to capture the true spirit within, I have also indulged myself in utilizing unusual views and the distorting effect of wide-angle lenses to create more than purely historic, visual recordings. Interpreted in my own photographic style, the results are (for me) beautiful and powerful pictures that I hope will reflect the outstanding beauty of the original subject.

Stella was right. There certainly is a book in Harrods and, now that it is complete, I can truly say that it has been one of the most enjoyable, satisfying and surprisingly dynamic that I've produced. The subject has been fascinating, the photographic opportunities bountiful and the 'team spirit' of the many thousands who work at Harrods uplifting. I truly hope that I have been successful in capturing the spirit of Harrods and encapsulating it in this book.

I also hope that *Harrods: Behind the Scenes* will help focus your attention not just on the merchandise but on Harrods itself: Harrods the building and the beautiful and magnificent opulence housed within. Such can only enhance your enjoyment of the world's most exciting shopping experience. Creating the imagery certainly has for me.

Chris Bennett, Oxted, October 1999

Harrods is the world's most famous luxury department store, selling highly desirable goods in opulent surroundings to customers who will have come from all corners of the globe simply to see and be seen at Harrods. Yet the store began as a small grocery shop, a sharp contrast to its later flamboyance and fame.

Charles Henry Harrod, a wholesale grocer and tea merchant since 1834, was increasingly drawn to a struggling grocery venture in Knightsbridge, owned by his customer and friend, Philip Henry Burden. By 1849, Harrod was in charge. Harrod's industry and prudence turned the business around, and soon it began to make a modest profit. The gradual development towards a department store was driven by the energy and enterprise of his son, Charles Digby Harrod, who snapped up adjoining properties, thereby gaining the space to expand the range of goods. New stock included necessities such as medicines, stationery and china. By the 1880s, Harrods Stores had a good reputation and a loyal clientele.

This was the business as Charles Digby Harrod sold it in 1889 – solid, reputable but lacking glamour. The new Managing Director, Richard Burbidge, had an eye for the grander possibilities. The 1890s saw a flurry of activity as Harrods transformed itself from a minor player to London's leading department store. Burbidge used his charm to persuade neighbouring businesses to sell their leases to Harrods, dramatically increasing the store's space. Most of Harrods familiar departments opened in this decade, alongside some that have not survived, for example, the forage, military equipment and mourning departments. Behind the scenes, too, Burbidge pioneered a new, more paternalistic approach to staff welfare, ensuring that employees had regular meals, shorter working hours and a range of leisure activities.

As the neighbouring properties were being acquired, a new building took shape. Its architecture reflected the store's fashionable image. The Edwardian opulence of the terracotta façade concealed interiors of unprecedented lavishness, such as the tiled food hall and rococco plasterwork of the fashion departments. Other stores had nothing to compare with this and visiting American warehousemen were aghast at the expenditure – but Burbidge knew what he was doing. Harrods immediately became one of the sights of London – it still is today.

'Everything London' was Harrods new telegraphic address. The idea that Harrods could provide everything for everybody everywhere, is one of Burbidge's most enduring legacies. At the same time, the store sought to be the epitome of style, selling the best quality goods to high society. Balancing these two different aims – universality versus exclusivity – continues to be a source of creative tension and stimulation for those managing the store's fortunes.

Harrods place as Society's favourite store and an English institution was not in any doubt for the first part of the twentieth century. By Harrods seventy-fifth anniversary, the store was receiving over 10,000 letters a year and was busy designing a new, classical exterior to the Basil Street frontage. While the 1930s Depression spelt leaner times for the store, albeit temporarily, the impact of the Second World War was much longer lasting. Rationing, evacuation to the countryside or abroad, together with reduced levels of public transport meant that fewer customers were coming into Harrods and, once in store, there was much less for them to spend their money on. Parts of the building were relinquished for military use – the Royal Navy and Royal Canadian Air Force moved in – while the store's civilian staff turned their hands to making uniforms, parachutes and parts for Lancaster bomber aeroplanes. The building itself survived the war largely unscathed.

It took years for Harrods to regain its swing after the Second World War. There was little money available for refurbishment or modernisation and visitors would, perhaps, have reflected that the store had seen better days. Instead of improvements, Harrods embarked on a spending spree, buying up bomb-damaged provincial stores such as John Walsh in Sheffield and Rackhams in Birmingham. Over-stretched resources made Harrods a vulnerable target and, in 1959, the Harrods Group was taken over by the House of Fraser.

Thirty-five years later, Harrods gained a new owner, Mohamed Al Fayed, and with this, new energies. Affection and money have been lavished on the store, enabling Harrods to carry out a programme of renovation, expansion and modernisation. The glamour has been heightened with innovative designs such as the breathtaking Egyptian escalators. With its worldwide reputation and wealth of experience, Harrods looks to the future with confidence.

Harrods is one of London's largest stores and key tourist attractions. But, way back in 1849, when he acquired a tiny grocer's shop in Brompton Road, Charles Henry Harrod could never have dreamed of the expansion that would occur over the years, nor indeed the fame and celebrity his name would hold. By the end of the nineteenth century, firstly under Charles's son, Charles Digby Harrod, and then with even more ferocity under Richard Burbidge – appointed General Manager in 1891 – Harrods was expanding rapidly, until finally, following extensive and complete redevelopment in 1905, transforming into the terracotta palace seen today.

It was a five-year development, completed in sections to permit trading to continue in those areas either renovated or unrenovated. Originally, only the first two floors of the new magnificent Knightsbridge landmark were for business use, the remaining three above being stylish residential apartments. The last of these was converted for Harrods trading in the 1970s.

The typical bustling London scene, looking down Knightsbridge from the south west, with Hans Road unseen to the right.

Majestic giant buglers herald in 1999, Harrods 150th year of trading.

A capital sight: the baroque dome on Harrods roof is a London landmark. In actual fact this masterpiece of elegance was built mostly for show, originally containing nothing more than a water tank.

High up beneath the baroque dome at the centre of the Harrods façade, Britannia, bronze trident at the ready, is offered produce (traditional grocers' produce, please note!), as she sits proudly upon the store's motto, 'Omnia Omnibus Ubique' – 'Everything for Everybody Everywhere'.

Sadly, due to its position, invisible to most shoppers, this elegant terracotta-faced chimney lances the deep blue London sky from the roof of Harrods.

As with many big city buildings, pigeons can be a problem, the many ledges, protrusions and recesses making ideal perches. To help discourage the permanent residence of such feathered friends, every couple of weeks a bird of prey is employed (very effectively) to deter loitering. The wire hanging down from this Harris Hawk is attached to a radio tracker – just in case he proves reluctant to return!

As the Sale draws near, its presence is proclaimed by immense gleaming white flags at the corners of Harrods roof. Beneath, the white spots are in fact a few of the 12,000 light bulbs that adorn the façade. When illuminated after dark, they give the building an almost fairytale effect.

Unseen by prospective bargain-hunting shoppers who will pound the floors in less than 24 hours, areas such as china and glassware appear chaotic while in preparation for the Sale. Here, expensive crystal is piled high in expectation of a brisk trade at substantially reduced prices.

For those with a penchant for rugs, heaven is at Harrods — or it will be once all those colourful floor coverings from around the globe are finally tidied in readiness for Sale time.

18

King of the bone china mountain, a handmade and decorated £750 (sale price!) Wedgwood teapot.

Mark Yacoob piles the Wedgwood high. His confident, almost casual, manner in dealing with such delicate and expensive items of china has been acquired through 20 years' experience in the Harrods Wedgwood Department.

There are certain areas in the store that are renowned for the ferocity of the hunt. Gucci bags is one; men's ties and sunglasses are others; and then there's women's shoes! Such a tidy, orderly start to the day, it's sad that it ends in such chaos once the Sale begins!

The horses and carriages are ready, Boyzone have arrived and the ever-efficient Press Office crew is in attendance. Anticipation grows as the Sale draws near. Situated opposite the main store, across the Brompton Road, Trevor Square, in addition to housing the stables, is also a goods receiving bank and depot for local deliveries around London – some performed by horse and carriage. Originally it housed factories for the production of luggage, chocolate and confectionery. Tea blending, coffee roasting and silversmithing, among other skills, were also carried out there.

Mmmm … they all look so tasty! Aboard the landau carriage in Trevor Square, Ronan Keating of Boyzone indulges in a little early morning Harrods hospitality.

24

Away from the public gaze within the confines of
Trevor Square, Cher finds time to sign a few autographs for
privileged fans and Green Men alike. International personalities
are invited to open the Harrods Sale, thus helping to attract
valuable publicity both for Harrods and the 'star' concerned.

Flanked by Green Men, Harrods bespoke doormen, and with David West at the reins, Boyzone use the original beautifully renovated 1880s landau carriage for the short transit from Trevor Square to Door 5 in Hans Crescent.

The action is in Hans Crescent at Door 5 and media attention is focused upon Chairman Al Fayed as he greets Cher who will, shortly, open the Sale...

…But, before going in, there's just time for Cher and Mr Al Fayed
to welcome personally the hordes of queuing bargain hunters.

Mohamed Al Fayed with chart-topping Irish pop band Boyzone.

When celebrities such as Cher or Boyzone are invited to open the biannual Harrods Sale, excitement is the order of the day. Press and fans test the carrying capacity of one of the Egyptian escalators in hot pursuit of Cher and Chairman Al Fayed, whilst a lone gentleman, remaining suitably detached from the fray, descends on the other.

Eager bargain hunters wait in anticipation as the countdown to the Harrods Sale leads to the calm before the …

... storm! On the first Saturday of the Sale the store expects some 300,000 bargain hunters through its doors. That's about ten times the normal daily average.

'There is only one Sale ...' (well, two
actually, because it's biannual) and Harrods
is the bargain hunters' paradise.

Such is the ferocity of the Sale that on the first Saturday all Harrods staff — even the directors — are called upon to lend a hand on the shop floor. Director Raine Spencer enjoys the ambience and excitement of the day as she does her bit in Cosmetics.

I wonder how many of those famous green and gold bags are dispensed on the first Saturday? It was in 1930 that these world-recognized carriers were first introduced — but then only for the Harrods Sale, another 43 years passing before they were issued for standard everyday use.

The Sale can be a serious adrenalin-generating event and, once you've claimed your silk ties, the frustration is in competing with your many fellow hunters for service. After all, time is of the essence as there are still unclaimed prizes to be had out there.

As predicted, Ladies' Shoes has degenerated into chaos, but at least staff and hunters are unanimous in their happiness.

The brainchild of Chairman Al Fayed, Harrods spectacular, ornate and colourful Egyptian escalators were designed by Bill Mitchell, the store's architect, and unveiled in 1997 after a construction cost of over £20 million. Of this princely sum, only £1 million went on the seven pairs of mobile stairways themselves, the remaining £19 million being spent on the magnificent setting in which they are located.

The subjects depicted on the friezes that adorn the walls about the escalators relate to the goods sold on that floor. This hunting and harvesting scene, for instance, indicates that it is not too far removed from the Food Halls.

42

This beautifully crafted stained glass ceiling panel is available for all who travel on the Egyptian escalators to admire, and it is well worth pausing (without holding up the passage of fellow shoppers) to study. In addition to being artistically splendid, the decoration surrounding the escalators does have a serious interpretation, the many paintings, hieroglyphics and sculptures being facsimiles of those found in eighteenth-dynasty ancient Egypt.

High up on the fifth floor ceiling is this beautiful, colourful astronomical relief of the night sky, complete with the signs of the zodiac depicted in gold – a fittingly spectacular culmination to the Harrods Egyptian escalator trail.

No expense has been spared to ensure that a visit to Harrods is an experience – an event – much more than just a shopping trip. There can be few halls in any shop as memorable as the Egyptian Hall at Harrods, mimicking as it does the splendour of the Kingdom of the Nile, the Pharaohs, sphinxes and temples of eighteenth-dynasty ancient Egypt.

Perhaps it is one's imagination, but the many bronzed
sphinxes that gaze defiantly down bear a striking
resemblance to benefactor Mohamed Al Fayed.

Elegance, style and
beauty are everywhere
at Harrods, the classic
symmetry of the
Egyptian Halls being a
photographer's dream.

Conscious of the hefty responsibility of its own heritage, the
Harrods Archive team is meticulous in the preservation of and
care for many historical documents and artefacts reflecting one
and a half centuries of Harrods trading.

The Archive exists to preserve fascinating but often delicate items of memorabilia such as this Inter-Season List from September 1895.

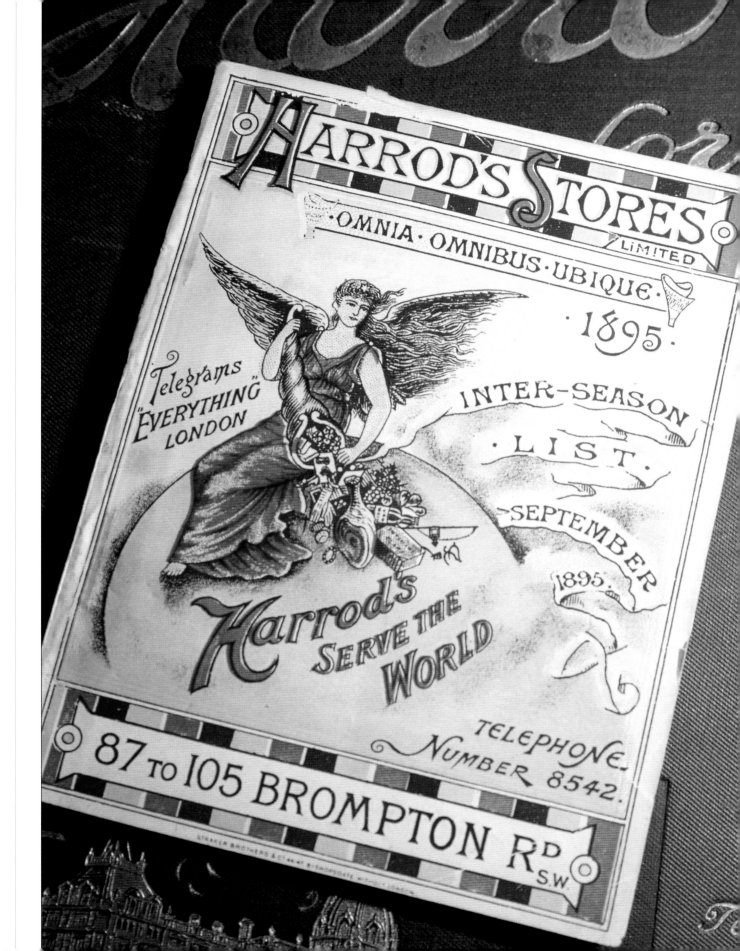

HARROD
LIMITED
—
REPORT
BOOK

No. 9

An example of the superbly designed stained glass on display, this depicting Harrods own coat of arms, granted in 1991. It looks old, but is actually a modern piece.

Housed in stables beneath the store's Trevor Square buildings, away from the public gaze, are Harrods magnificent Friesian horses. When not in service in London, the horses take respite from the hustle and bustle of the capital at the Chairman's countryside residence in Oxted, Surrey.

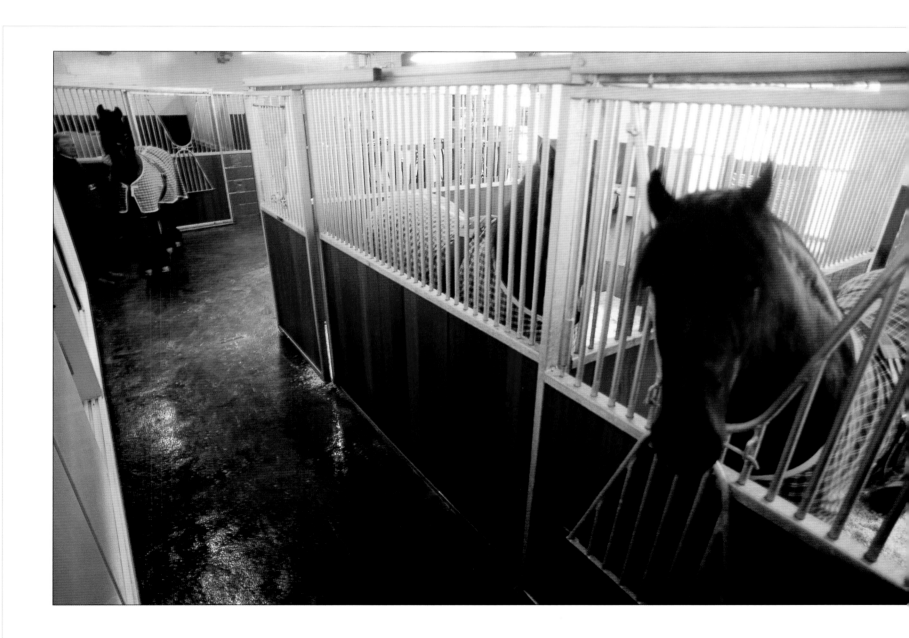

Harrods coach and horses team is often to be seen competing at equestrian events and country shows nationwide. Even away from London, carrying the prestigious Harrods banner for quality – presentation and meticulous attention to detail is all important.

David West and his team are devoted to
the eight Dutch Friesians in their care
and you will not see more immaculately
groomed horses anywhere.

Heads and hooves high, the Harrods coach and horses add a touch of class and spectacle wherever they appear, their labours being rewarded by the growing number of trophies and rosettes in the cabinet.

In fact, judging by the red and white ribbon that adorns this bridle,

their endeavours have proved fruitful once again.

Buckingham Palace and the Victoria Monument recede into the distance as the Harrods Friesians, carriage in tow, clip-clop majestically down the Mall. The carriages are frequently used for central London deliveries to venues such as palaces and hotels. They may not be one of the swiftest modes of delivery, but, when speed is not of the essence, they are the most stylish.

A London cab whizzes by as David brings the Friesians to a halt opposite the National Gallery. To their right, unseen, are Trafalgar Square and Nelson's Column, but it is guaranteed that when the coach and horses trot around the square, the battery of tourists' cameras will be focused on them.

Rodney is a veteran of 44 years' service, and therefore one of
Harrods longest-serving members of staff. When not running
messages for the Chairman, he occasionally pops out with the
horse and carriage to help make local central London deliveries.
Harrods own Fashion Department was responsible for making
Rodney's coat, ideal for the more inclement months.

Except for the 'bus lane' and the modern vehicles in the background, this could almost be a scene from nineteenth-century London as, late one November afternoon, the Harrods Friesians negotiate Westminster Bridge.

67

An early morning trip to Billingsgate Fish Market provides the ultra-fresh produce with which to replenish the Food Hall's fish counters. Restocking commences at around 7am and must be completed, with everything tidied and all surfaces and floors polished, for the doors to open at 10am.

At Harrods, there is an impressively high level of presentation in the daily ritual of the restocking of the Food Halls.

Harrods is famous for its Food Halls and the splendid array of produce to be found there, everything for any gastronomic occasion. From the humble potato (the very best quality, of course) to Italian white truffles at around £250 per 100g or a £5,000 bottle of Château Cheval Blanc 1947, Harrods really can supply 'Everything for Everybody Everywhere'!

A bird's-eye view of early morning preparations. Within the hour, this scene of orderly chaos will transform into one of orderly perfection, when the Harrods Florists conjure up some spectacular floral arrangements, the scent of blooms adding to the overall aroma of freshness in the Food Halls.

Prior to opening, final preparations
are made at the ground floor
bakery. Many of the 150 types of
bread available will have been
baked during the wee small hours
in the store's own ovens.

It is around 9.45am, a quarter of an hour before opening, and preparations at the Pizzeria are in full swing. The myriad of ingredients are sliced and diced and dough is mixed (the constituents of which are a closely guarded secret) in anticipation of a busy morning and hectic lunchtime ahead.

With the deft touch of the master,
Giuseppe spins a dough base aloft.
This action removes the surplus flour
that might spoil the finished pizza.
Customers of the Harrods Pizzeria
are often entertained as they eat with
this practical showmanship.

Giuseppe, a man with a passion for pizza, ladles one of his mouth-watering creations into the 600-degree wood-fired oven.

At Harrods – and perhaps especially in the Food Halls – spectacle is supreme. To maintain such a level of tidy elegance the stock is constantly (but discreetly) rearranged or replenished throughout the day to keep that fresh, 10 o'clock, just-opened look. In essence, the Food Halls look today as they would have after construction in 1903. However, their splendour was for many years hidden, the tiled surfaces being boarded up in the late 1940s, only to be uncovered again nearly 40 years later.

81

The Sea Grill offers a safe port amid the shopping storm.

Both the sweet and the savoury tooth are catered for in the extensive Food Halls. Historically, food is at the very heart of Harrods – it did, after all, start as a small grocer's shop – and food (whether the purchase of or the consumption of) is still the store's principal emphasis.

Apart from being a mine of London knowledge and custodian of the doors, since the early 1900s the Harrods Green Man has provided a welcome touch of gentlemanly courtesy so often lacking in today's hectic times. Mrs Thompson, a stalwart Harrods customer now in her nineties, is offered a helping hand along Hans Crescent from Bob, en route to Door 5.

Introduced by Chairman Al Fayed, the Pipers' daily walkabout has become a celebrated tradition. The tartan they wear belongs to the Clan Ross, whose family seat, Balnagown, is now owned by Mr Al Fayed.

86

On most days, when his hectic schedule permits, Mr Al Fayed
will personally walk around the store to keep an eye on the
running of his 'ship'. A casual chat with customers is a good
way to make sure that their needs are being met by Harrods.

To be found in the
Food Halls,
meticulously
sculpted mermaids
entice shoppers
to partake of
their wares.

An ornate dispenser gives the purchase of coffee, an outwardly mundane task, a characteristically Harrods air of theatre. As befits a store which began its life as a grocer's shop, Harrods has a huge range of coffees – over 30 varieties – and an even greater selection of teas – 151 types, including one specially blended to provide a brew that commemorates the shop's first 150 years of trading.

Many of the more popular coffees offered for sale are kept fresh in towering, sealed, copper dispensers.

89

One of the Food Halls
traditionally attired
assistants dispenses tea in
the appropriate time-
honoured manner — after
all, tea blending was one of
Charles Henry Harrod's
first endeavours.

Expensive delicacies such as wild boar can be found in the
Food Halls for those with a taste for such exotic fare.

In the Fromagerie, up to
350 different cheeses are
available, a formidable choice
guaranteed to satisfy even the
most discerning of palates.

The Rotisserie, one of the handful of café bars situated within or adjacent to the Food Halls. Many of the restaurants and bars within Harrods are relatively recent additions, installed in the early to mid-1990s, providing within one building a vast and unique panorama of culinary diversification.

At the colourful Candy Bar
you'll find over 50 flavours of
Jelly Bellys – one to suit all tastes!

The simple elegance and colour of traditional Japanese dishes are available
at the Sushi Bar, catering for the many Japanese visitors to Harrods and
those with a taste for adventure who perhaps reside more locally.

Food Halls visited and delicacies purchased and
packed, Mrs Thompson is bid a hearty farewell
as Bob prepares to see her safely home.

The old Harrods trademark and slogan 'Harrods Serve the World' was adopted by General Manager Richard Burbidge in the early 1890s.

The large polished cauldrons
of the production kitchens
provide the facilities to cook
asparagus in serious volume.

With the exception of The Georgian Restaurant which has its own dedicated kitchen and those self-contained restaurants such as the Pizzeria and the Rotisserie, all of the extensive items of food production emanate from the scrupulously clean main production kitchens. In essence, the highly efficient production kitchens are made up of four individual areas: those producing hot and cold food, the pastry kitchen and the bakery. In addition to all manner of other gastronomic delights great and small, the production kitchens are responsible for delivering some 3,000 sandwiches and up to 10,000 staff meals every working day.

In Harrods main production kitchens – as everywhere else – expertise and creativity play
their part. The quality and artistry of the fruit carving could not be surpassed.

A dish is flambéed in the smaller, dedicated
Georgian Restaurant kitchen.

A first-rate example of fruit carving, a decorative art that is
enthusiastically practised at Harrods. Sadly, within a week this
masterpiece, carved from a watermelon, will be fit only for the bin.

Boasting some 20 restaurants, Harrods
choice is second to none. For those
wishing to dine in traditional elegance,
The Georgian Restaurant is the order of
the day, here seen adorned with 150th
anniversary celebratory garlands. The
Georgian Restaurant has existed since
1911 and is one of the biggest shop-based
restaurants in the world.

The resplendent
Georgian Restaurant
where refined
surroundings and serene
melodies are matched
only by the culinary
delights available therein.

The Georgian Restaurant in full cry.

Among the extensive suites of offices on the fifth floor is the boardroom where, on a regular basis, the directors of Harrods congregate to discuss matters of business import.

Weighing in at over 25 tons apiece, Harrods has a battery of nine massive electricity generators, three situated in the sub-basement beneath the store and the remaining six beneath Trevor Square. Each producing 8.4MVA, these generators are more than capable of supplying enough current for all the store's extensive power requirements, making Harrods, if necessary, self-sufficient. Normally, however, only half of them are in operation at any one time, these supplying 50 per cent of the store's electricity, the balance coming from the National Grid.

In control: extra power,
heat and water for Harrods
at the flick of a switch.

Health and fitness amongst staff
is important. One of Harrods
team of fire-fighters takes his
annual physical.

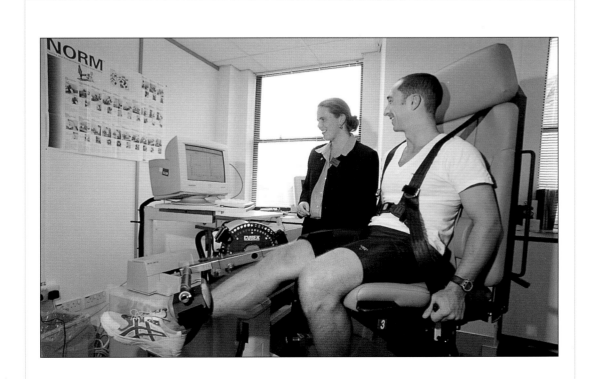

Total Calls = 7162

Upgraded in 1997, the central switchboard at Brompton Place receives some 12,000 calls per day on their 350 incoming lines. They take pride in the minimal number of calls lost and the accumulated tally received, a constantly updated record of which can be seen on the wall in the background.

Harrods take their security – both merchandise and customer safety – very seriously indeed. Their highly-trained security officers are ever-present on the shop floor and in constant two-way radio contact with HQ, where an awesome bank of monitors give the big picture.

Constructed in 1989 at a cost of £30 million, the Harrods
warehouse and distribution centre at Osterley near Heathrow is
one of the most advanced in the world and can facilitate the
storage of over four million items of stock. Outside, awaiting
deliveries, is a selection of Harrods vehicles, including charismatic
petrol-driven replicas of the original electric 1919 Walker vans.

It is at the warehouse that much of the packaging and storage of goods prior to despatch to Knightsbridge or directly to purchasers' private residences is accomplished.

As soon as stocks are depleted from the shelves in Knightsbridge, they are replenished, often from the store's Osterley warehouse. A computerized logging system enables items to be quickly located and removed from the massive 'shelving' unit in High Bay.

Small and delicate items are bubble-wrapped and boxed before delivery.

Harrods takes customer and staff safety very
seriously and many of the staff are trained in
basic fire-fighting techniques. In addition to
practical instruction in the use of various types
of extinguishers, they get to try their hands at
rescuing a body (or in this case a realistically
weighted dummy!) from a smoke-filled room.

At Osterley, the traditional skills of the furniture- and cabinet-maker are alive and well. Here a settee is being modified, the hand-finished, personal touch making it just that little bit better than when it left the manufacturer, while in the workshops some new custom-made display counters destined for Knightsbridge are under construction.

Gathering dust in the Osterley workshops, these colourful and gallant wooden soldiers are retired from the front-line. But if duty calls and their presence is required to add character to Harrods, they'll not be found wanting.

For those with a purpose, a visit to the subterranean world of Harrods safety deposit is a time-transportation back to the 1890s, when the 2,600 safety deposit boxes and 13 strong rooms were first made and installed. They are the oldest original part of the store, the safes and strong room being purchased for the then substantial sum of £1,650 from Ratners of Glasgow in 1896. Although most definitely atmospheric, the Harrods vaults are a rather claustrophobic environment in which to work. But manager Colin Dalman takes such a metallic encasement in his stride – he used to be a submariner! In fact Colin spent nine years serving in submarines, two of which were in HMS *Dreadnought*, the Royal Navy's first nuclear powered submarine.

Stylish architecture abounds within Harrods which boasts perhaps
the most resplendent bank entrance to be found anywhere.

A banking hall has existed at Harrods since 1890. Situated on the lower ground, the present hall was constructed in 1989, its characterful Edwardian style lending a much earlier feel.

In the hallowed halls of the Harrods Fine Jewellery Room can be found some of the most spectacular jewellery and watches ever crafted, from the world's finest makers. This Piaget timepiece – an 18 carat gold square galaxy bracelet watch – is set with 316 diamonds and can be yours for a mere £530,000.

Ladies with a penchant for pampering need look no further than Harrods Hair and Beauty Salon. This is the view when one first enters the department, the openness and symmetry somehow befitting a location for beautification.

The inner sanctum of the
Ladies Hair and Beauty
Salon, the lofty ceiling
and Romano style pillars
add to the bright
spaciousness within.

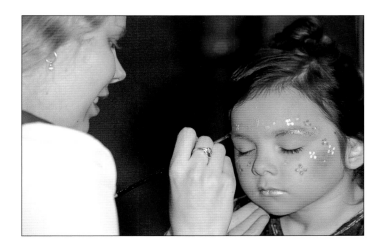

For boys and girls lighter in years, for whom beautification is not yet a problem, face painting in the surroundings of the Children's Hairdressers has a whole other meaning.

All animals sold in the Harrods Pet Department are thoroughly inspected by the store's vet, just to make sure they are as bright eyed and bushy tailed as they should be before beginning a new life outside Knightsbridge.

Teddy bears have become a tradition at Harrods, are available in all shapes and sizes and made from a variety of materials – including china.

Principally with the younger shopper in
mind (or perhaps the young at heart),
Planet Harrods is the extrovert venue for
a juicy hamburger with fries on the side.

Those wishing an informal pint in an old English tavern need not venture out into the streets, for a warm welcome is sure to be found in Harrods very own Green Man pub where, for a modest sum, a pint of Harrods ale can be purchased. In Jacobean style, the Green Man is one of Harrods earliest (and most unique) food and drink outlets, being a 1973 conversion of the old barber shop waiting room.

Take the escalator down to the lower ground and the Wine Department, and on your left is one of two cigar outlets where the finest of Havanas can be purchased. These outlets are in fact run for Harrods by J J Fox of St James's, a bespoke tobacconist and a company whose origins reach as far back as Harrods.

Amongst the extensive selection of Havanas available in Harrods is the Cohiba brand, arguably the finest and certainly one of the most expensive cigars in the world. Initially produced exclusively for the personal enjoyment of President Fidel Castro, it was not until 1982 that the relatively young brand of Cohiba was offered for sale to lesser mortals.

On the lower ground floor, near the Wine Department and opposite Cigars, an Iberian welcome can be found in the heart of London's Knightsbridge at the Tapas Bar.

One of the gentlemen's rest rooms, a suitably elegant respite in 'shoppers' heaven'.

Celebrities and fashion hounds of all types flock to Harrods.

Catwalk presentations are a
regular part of the fashion
calendar at Harrods.
Attended by top models
and the world's press, the
leading fashion houses use
them as a high-profile
opportunity to present
their latest creations.

145

Cameras whirl as celebrity designer John Galliano mingles during one of the many fashion evenings at Harrods. The model on John's right wears a specially created dress that was later auctioned, the proceeds going to charity.

Harrods hosts quite a number of fashion events each year, varying from stylish catwalk presentations (often put on in conjunction with such notables as *Elle* magazine), to 'meet and greets' with the likes of John Galliano or Michael Kors, designer for the Celine label.

Appropriately stylish food fuels those who come to Harrods for the many fashion events it hosts. Here, after closing hours, during an early evening show, the store's adaptable chefs utilise the first floor Ladies Shoes Department as a temporary base for their operations, from which to serve previously prepared canapés and other gastronomic delicacies

Canapés devoured, champagne sipped, the fashion show is coming to a close and guests are wending their way home. Soon they will be followed by this gaggle of highly experienced Harrods chefs. But they'll be back bright and early to help feed the many visitors who flock to Knightsbridge.

Richard E. Grant on the publicity trail.

Harrods Book Department often sees visits from celebrity authors who, if you join the queue and ask politely, will sign a valued book for you. 'So you'd just like "With best wishes, David Attenborough?".'

Ever the English rose, Joan Collins arrives at Door 10 in Hans Road. Her new book has just been launched and a press laden signing session at Harrods is a good way to drum up extra publicity.

Joan Collins in the spotlight at Harrods. While the public waits, the press have a few minutes to snap their pictures and ask a few questions before being politely ushered away, at which time the signing session can commence in earnest.

Mr Al Fayed always tries to greet the Harrods guests personally. His delight at receiving a signed copy of Joan Collins's *My Friends' Secrets* is plain for all to see.

The Christmas windows at Harrods really are superbly stylish and beautiful, taking much meticulous planning and design. The window display team are used to being in the public eye as they put the very final touches of perfection on their elegant creations.

Christmas decorative effects are unique to each department. In the Cosmetics Department, appropriate subtlety, brightness and crispness are the results.

Christmas comes but once a year and Harrods partakes enthusiastically in the festive spirit. The snow may be artificial at the Harrods Christmas Parade, but the joy and air of fantasy it brings to young and old are not.

Using the store's collection of wonderful, gleaming original carriages, the Christmas Parade travels down Brompton Road, around Hans Road and the back of Harrods, into the snow-scape of Hans Crescent, where, at the vanguard, the Pipers call all to attention, for Santa is on his way.

The culmination of the Harrods Christmas Parade is the arrival of Santa from Lapland. The worry is, with such a long distance to cover, will he arrive on time? But miraculously and with faithful reindeer Donner and Blitzen at the fore (and perhaps after a pitstop at Trevor Square for a warming glass of mulled wine!) somehow, to the delight of all, he does!

Once Santa is known to be in the area, there's usually time before he lands for the Harrods horses to display their charms. As the Dutch Friesians bring up the rear amidst the falling snow, David West's wife, Sarah, leads the parade with the 'Oh so cute', pint-sized Shetland ponies.

On arrival in Hans Crescent and after a warm welcome from Mr Al Fayed, Santa does what
Santa does best – bringing delight to the hearts of little children (and some big children, too!).

Christmas is for children, big and small, young and old, and a trip along to the Harrods Grotto to meet Santa personally is a must. But, with an average of 35,000 children accompanied by 15,000 parents knocking on his door each Christmas, do allow plenty of time, as the red-coated, silver-bearded Laplander is in huge demand.

Christmas partying: Harrods staff, who heroically assist shoppers in preparing for December festivities, enjoy themselves down the road from Knightsbridge at the Dorchester.

At Harrods there is always a familiar welcome and a friendly goodbye at every door. And you never know, it might even be the Chairman himself who says, '*Thank you for shopping at Harrods!*'